THE MEANING OF SHIT

Summersdale Publishers Ltd
46 West Street
Chichester
West Sussex
PO19 1RP
UK

www.summersdale.com

Printed and bound in the Czech Republic

ISBN: 978-1-84953-502-1

Substantial discounts on bulk quantities of Summersdale books are available to corporations, professional associations and other organisations. For details contact Nicky Douglas by telephone: +44 (0) 1243 756902, fax: +44 (0) 1243 786300 or email: nicky@summersdale.com.

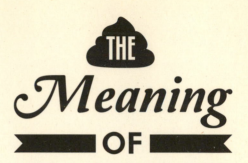

THE Meaning OF SHIT

THE Meaning OF SHIT

A Scatalogicon

summersdale

CONTENTS

RELIGIOUS SHIT

TAOISM

• •

Shit happens.

CONFUCIANISM

• •

Confucius say,
'Shit happens.'

BUDDHISM

••••••••••••••••••••••••••••

*If shit happens,
it isn't really shit.*

ZEN

· ·

What is the sound of

shit happening?

HINDUISM

· ·

This shit has

happened before.

HARE KRISHNA

· ·

Shit happens, shit
happens, happens,
happens, shit, shit...

SIKHISM

· ·

This shit was revealed

by the Guru.

CATHOLICISM

· ·

If shit happens,
you deserved it.

PROTESTANTISM

· ·

If shit happens,
praise the Lord for it!

FUNDAMENTALISM

....

*If shit happens, you
will go to hell, unless
you are born again.*

JEHOVAH'S WITNESSES

....

*Good morning,
I have some shit for
you to read.*

AMISH

· ·

*This modern shit
is immoral.*

JUDAISM

• •

So shit happens,
already!

ISLAM

· ·

There is no shit
but shit.

NEW AGE

· ·

If shit happens,
honour it and share it.

VOODOO

....

Let's stick pins

in this shit!

SATANISM

·····························

Shit happens.

JEDI

· ·

May the shit
be with you.

AGNOSTICISM

· ·

*How can we KNOW
if shit happens?*

ATHEISM

....

I don't believe

this shit!

··················

PHILOSOPHICAL SHIT

EXISTENTIALISM

· ·

Shit happening is
absurd.

FATALISM

· ·

Shit is going

to happen.

FEMINISM

· ·

We want the same

shit as men.

FETISHISM

. . . .

I love it when

shit happens.

HEDONISM

. . . .

*There's nothing quite
like a good shit.*

MASOCHISM

• •

Shit on me.

SADISM

· ·

I will shit on you.

OPTIMISM

....

This shit is

pretty good.

PESSIMISM

· ·

Shit sucks.

NIHILISM

· ·

This shit has

no meaning.

POLITICAL CORRECTNESS

....

Heavily processed

waste matter

discharged from the

bowels happens.

PROCRASTINATION

· ·

I'll shit tomorrow.

STOICISM

· ·

This shit doesn't

hurt at all.

VEGETARIANISM

· ·

If it shits,
don't eat it.

THALES

· ·

*Earth, Air, Fire
and Shit.*

SOCRATES

....

What is shit?

Why is shit?

EPICURUS

· ·

If shit happens,
enjoy it.

ARCHIMEDES

· ·

Hmm... why
doesn't this shit float?

RENÉ DESCARTES

• •

I shit, therefore I am.

FRIEDRICH NIETZSCHE

· ·

Shit is dead.

SIGMUND FREUD

· ·

Shit is a
phallic symbol.

JEAN-PAUL SARTRE

· ·

Shit is other people.

KURT GÖDEL

· ·

It can be proved that it

cannot be proved that

shit happens.

SCIENTIFIC
SHIT

ASTRONOMER

· ·

*Look at all that shit
in the sky.*

BIOLOGIST

• •

Is this shit alive?

CHEMIST

....

I hope this shit

doesn't blow up.

DOCTOR

. . . .

Take two shits and call

me in the morning.

ENGINEER

• •

*I hope this shit
holds together.*

MATHEMATICIAN

·······················

You can't divide

shit by zero.

PHYSICIST (THEORETICAL)

·······················

Shit SHOULD

happen.

PHYSICIST
(EXPERIMENTAL)

. . . .

To within

experimental error,

shit DID happen.

PSYCHOLOGIST

· ·

And how did that shit make you feel?

SURGEON

....

Shit, where's this organ supposed to go?

CHARLES DARWIN

• • • • • • • • • • • • • • • • • • • •

Survival of

the shittest.

ALBERT EINSTEIN

· ·

Shit is relative.

ERWIN SCHRÖDINGER

. . . .

This simultaneously is and is not shit.

WERNER HEISENBERG

· ·

Shit happened,
we just don't know
where or how much.

NEIL ARMSTRONG

· ·

One small shit for a man... One giant heap for mankind.

POLITICAL
SHIT

POLITICIAN

· ·

If you elect me,
shit will never
happen again.

COMMUNISM

. . . .

Share the shit equally.

CAPITALISM

····························

That's MY shit.

JULIUS CAESAR

· ·

I came, I saw,
I shitted.
(Veni, Vidi, Shitti.)

GEORGE WASHINGTON

• •

I cannot tell a lie –
shit happened.

ABRAHAM LINCOLN

. . . .

Four score and seven

shits ago...

FRANKLIN D. ROOSEVELT

· ·

*The only thing
we have to fear
is shit itself.*

JOHN F. KENNEDY

· ·

Ask not what your shit can do for you; ask what you can do for your shit.

BILL CLINTON

•••••••••••••••••••••••

I didn't inhale

this shit.

HENRY VIII

· ·

Off with their shit!

WINSTON CHURCHILL

. . . .

We shall shit on

the beaches.

MARGARET THATCHER

• •

The shit is not

for turning.

TONY BLAIR

· ·

*None of this shit
was my fault.*

DAVID CAMERON

• •

*We're all in this
shit together.*

SOCIAL SHIT

AIRHEAD

· ·

OMG, this shit is like totes amazing!

DYSLEXIC

• •

Tihs happens.

ENVIRONMENTALIST

· ·

Is that shit recycled?

FACEBOOK ADDICT

· ·

*Like and share
my shit!*

GOSSIP

· ·

Stir the shit up and
dish the shit out.

HIPSTER

....

I liked this shit before

it was cool.

POSER

· ·

I have the latest shit.

STUDENT

· ·

*I'll just sleep
through this shit.*

TWITTER ADDICT

· ·

*My shit's got
10,000 followers!*

VANDAL

....

Let's break some shit.

WORK SHIT

———————————

GOOD DAYS

· ·

I do this shit

for a living!

BAD DAYS

· ·

*I don't get paid
enough for this shit.*

APPRAISAL TIME

· ·

You're shit.

PAY NEGOTIATIONS

• •

You want HOW MUCH shit!?

ACCOUNTS

· ·

Your shit's

in the post.

ADMINISTRATION

. . . .

I'm sorry, but we can't make this shit happen until you fill out form XP1 in triplicate...

BLUE-SKY THINKING

· ·

I like to shit outside

the box.

HEALTH & SAFETY

· ·

Please keep

your shit tidy.

HUMAN RELATIONS

· ·

*We're looking
for continuous
improvement of
our shit.*

IT HELPDESK

. . . .

Have you tried restarting your shit?

MANAGEMENT

· ·

Shit harder!

MARKETING

· ·

This shit could sell,
if only it came in
different colours.

PAYROLL

· ·

You can have your

shit once a month.

CHEF

· ·

And some shit on the top to garnish.

DRIVING EXAMINER

· ·

When I tap on the dashboard, I would like you to do an emergency shit.

ECONOMIST

· ·

I hope no one realises that I don't really understand this shit.

HAIRDRESSER

· ·

*Whoever cut this last
time was shit.*

HISTORIAN

· ·

Shit repeats itself.

LAWYER

....

*For a sufficient fee,
I can get you out of
ANY shit.*

MECHANIC

. . . .

This shit's going

to cost you...

POLICE OFFICER

· ·

Anything you shit
may be given as
evidence in court.

TEACHER

· ·

Repeat after me:
one shit + one shit = ...

UNION LEADER

. . . .

Give us more shit or we'll strike.

WAITER

• •

You want fries with that shit?

CULTURAL
SHIT

BLUES MUSIC

· ·

Woke up this
morning, took a shit.

MINIMALISM

· ·

Shit.

PAINTING

. . . .

This is an
abstract shit.

POETRY

. . . .

The cat shat

on the mat.

ROCK MUSIC

· ·

This shit needs a solo.

SURREALISM

....

Fish.

LEONARDO DA VINCI

• •

Can you tell what this

shit is thinking?

WILLIAM SHAKESPEARE

....

To shit or not to shit,
that is the question.

JACKSON POLLOCK

· ·

This is what I call

action shitting.

CLARK GABLE

· ·

*Frankly, my dear,
I don't give a shit.*

GRETA GARBO

....

I want to shit alone.

FRANK SINATRA

. . . .

I shat it my way.

CAPTAIN JAMES T. KIRK

· ·

... to boldly shit where no man has shat before!

MR SPOCK

· ·

Shit long and prosper.

CLINT EASTWOOD

· ·

Do you feel shit,
punk?

ELVIS PRESLEY

· ·

Don't shit on my blue

suede shoes.

AL PACINO

• •

*Say hello to
my little shit.*

OTIS REDDING

· ·

Shitting on the

dock of the bay.

ARNOLD SCHWARZENEGGER

• •

Shit'll be back.

NOEL EDMONDS

....

Shit or no shit?

LIONEL RICHIE

· ·

Shitting on
the ceiling.

MR T

....

I pity the shit.

JAMES CAMERON

. . . .

This shit's expensive!

DAMIEN HIRST

• •

*You can cut a shit
in half, but it's still
a shit.*

MICHAEL BAY

· ·

Let's blow some

shit up.

BEYONCÉ

. . . .

*If you liked shit
you should have put
a ring on it.*

RIHANNA

· ·

The only shit

in the world.

ANIMAL SHIT

BEAR

· ·

*Do I shit in
the woods?*

CAT

· ·

Dogs are shit.

DOG

• •

I love all this shit!

DUNG BEETLE

. . . .

This shit tastes great.

ELEPHANT

· ·

An elephant never forgets to shit.

FISH

• •

All I do is eat,

swim and shit.

MEERKAT

....

Even my shit is cute!

PARROT

· ·

Who's a pretty shit?

SEAGULL

· ·

Watch out, here

comes my shit!

SEAHORSE

• •

*Whose shit idea was it
to single us guys out to
have the babies?*

SLOTH

....

I would shit but
I can't be bothered.

TORTOISE

· ·

*Slow and steady
wins the shit.*

If you're interested in finding out more about our shit,
find us on Facebook at Summersdale Publishers
and follow us on Twitter at @Summersdale.

www.summersdale.com